ENERGY REVOLUTION

GEOTHERMAL

ENERGY

By M. M. Eboch

raintree
a Capstone company — publishers for children

Raintree is an imprint of Capstone Global Library Limited, a company incorporated in England and Wales having its registered office at 264 Banbury Road, Oxford, OX2 7DY – Registered company number: 6695582

www.raintree.co.uk
myorders@raintree.co.uk

Edited by Mandy Robbins
Designed by Terri Poburka
Original illustrations © Capstone Global Library Limited 2020
Picture research by Jo Miller
Production by Kathy McColley
Originated by Capstone Global Library Ltd
Printed and bound in India

ISBN 978 1 4747 6989 1 (hardcover)
ISBN 978 1 4747 6995 2 (paperback)

British Library Cataloguing in Publication Data
A full catalogue record for this book is available from the Bri⌷

Acknowledgements
We would like to thank the following for permission to reproduce photographs: Alamy: Joerg Boethling, 21; AP Images: Jeff Barnard, 4; Newscom: ZUMA Press/Guiziou Franck, 11; Science Source: Claus Lunau, 22, Theodore Clutter, 25; Shutterstock: anyalvanova, 29, Designua, 9, Dhimas Adi Satrina, 18, Ellen Bronstayn, 6, EpicStockMedia, 23, Gary Whitton, 14, jjspring, 10, MarcelClemens, 17, Mehmet Cetin, 27, Palmi Gudmundsson, 12, Peter Gudella, Cover. Design Elements: Shutterstock: HAKKI ARSLAN, T.Sumaetho.

CONTENTS

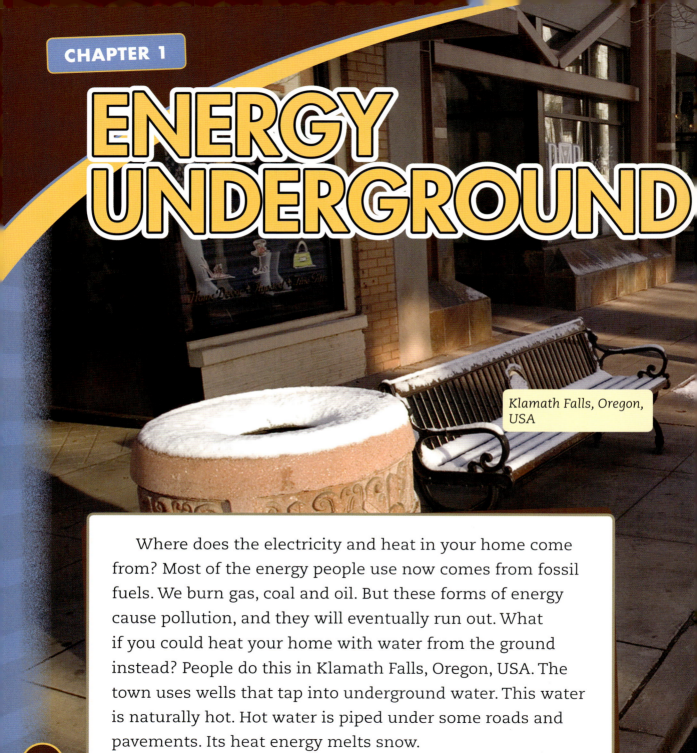

CHAPTER 1

ENERGY UNDERGROUND

Klamath Falls, Oregon, USA

Where does the electricity and heat in your home come from? Most of the energy people use now comes from fossil fuels. We burn gas, coal and oil. But these forms of energy cause pollution, and they will eventually run out. What if you could heat your home with water from the ground instead? People do this in Klamath Falls, Oregon, USA. The town uses wells that tap into underground water. This water is naturally hot. Hot water is piped under some roads and pavements. Its heat energy melts snow.

This energy also gets turned into electricity. It provides heat for homes, schools and a hospital. The energy also powers TVs, computers, cookers and much more. Using hot water for energy saves the town money. It also cuts down on pollution.

Heat from inside Earth is called **geothermal** energy. It is held in the rocks and water in the ground.

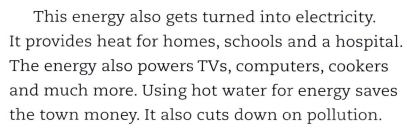

FACT

The word "geothermal" relates to the heat inside Earth. *Geo* refers to Earth. *Thermal* relates to heat or temperature.

RENEWABLE ENERGY

More than 75 per cent of the world's energy comes from fossil fuels. This percentage has been falling as people find alternatives. **Renewable** energy comes from nature. This may be heat from the Sun or motion from the wind. It may be **hydropower** or geothermal energy. This energy is turned into electrical energy. Then people can use the energy just as they would if it came from fossil fuels.

geothermal relating to the intense heat inside Earth

renewable describes power from sources that you can use again and again that cannot be used up, such as wind, water and the Sun

hydropower form of energy caused by flowing water

CHAPTER 2

HOW POWER STATIONS WORK

How does geothermal energy provide heat and electricity? Energy can change from one type to another.

A traditional power station uses coal, natural gas or oil. Workers burn these fuels to boil water. The boiling water turns into steam. As the steam moves through the air, it turns a large fan called a **turbine**. The fan's moving blades power a **generator**. This machine makes electricity by turning a magnet inside a coil of wire. The magnets change the movement into electrical energy. The electricity is sent through wires into homes and businesses.

FACT

Fossil fuels come from plants or animals that died millions of years ago. Coal, oil and natural gas are fossil fuels.

How a geothermal power station works

Geothermal power stations start with hot water or steam from deep within the earth. The heat is converted to electricity. Then the water is returned back to the earth.

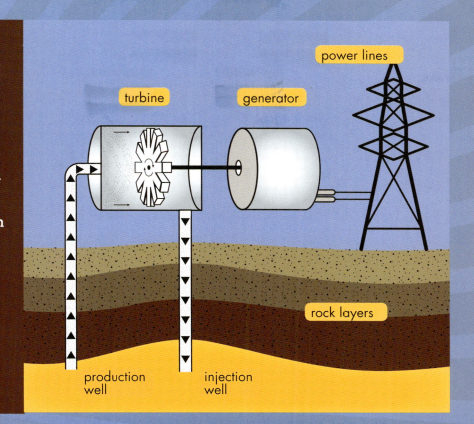

turbine

generator

power lines

rock layers

production well

injection well

Geothermal power stations skip the first step. They don't burn fuel in order to heat water. Instead they use boiling water or steam from inside the earth. Pumps bring fluid from deep underground to the surface. Then these power stations make electricity the same way as traditional ones. As they don't burn fossil fuels, this cuts down on pollution.

turbine machine with blades that can be turned by steam or water

generator machine used to convert mechanical energy into electricity

USING EARTH'S HEAT

Geothermal power stations need two things – water and heat. Earth's crust is about 24 to 56 kilometres (15 to 35 miles) thick on land. But in some places, the crust is thinner. In these cracks or channels, heat can rise towards the surface. Some places also have underground water. If the heat and water reach all the way to the surface, you may see hot springs. In these places it's easy to reach Earth's hot water.

Bathers enjoy the natural hot springs in the Atacama Desert in Bolivia.

People have visited hot springs since **ancient** times. They used the warm water for bathing, washing clothes and cooking. In 1904, an Italian prince found another use for hot springs. He trapped steam coming from the ground in a valley called Val di Cecina and used it to turn a small engine. This made enough electricity to light five light bulbs. He proved that the earth's heat could make electricity. People in Italy built a power station at that location in 1911. It was the first geothermal power station in the world. Today that station provides power to about 1 million homes.

ancient from a long time ago

The Larderello Val di Cecina geothermal power station uses Italy's natural hot springs.

ACCESSING GEOTHERMAL ENERGY

People in cities such as Klamath Falls, Oregon, USA, can easily use the earth's hot water. Iceland has a lot of geothermal activity too. People there have used water from hot springs for bathing, cooking and laundry for many years. Today about nine out of ten homes in Iceland use geothermal energy for heat. They even heat swimming pools with it. In Iceland geothermal energy creates 25 per cent of the country's electricity.

Not every country has hot springs. Those that do may have them only in a few places. Those places may be far from where people live. If people in places without hot springs want underground hot water, they have to dig for it. Geothermal power stations can be built in places without hot springs. They can work wherever Earth's crust is thin enough. Today companies can drill down 1.6 kilometres (1 mile) or more to reach deep hot water or steam.

The Blue Lagoon is a natural hot spring in Iceland.

CHAPTER 3

GEOTHERMAL PROS AND CONS

Coal-fired power stations release harmful chemicals into the air.

Geothermal power stations have advantages over power stations that burn fossil fuels. Using fossil fuels to make power causes a lot of pollution. When fossil fuels are burned, they release chemicals such as carbon dioxide. These chemicals can make people unwell and pollute lakes and rivers. They get into the air as greenhouse gases. The gases cause climate change, which causes rising sea levels and extreme weather. Geothermal power stations don't produce this pollution. They release 99 per cent less carbon dioxide than fossil fuel power stations.

Geothermal energy is also renewable. These power stations remove hot water from the ground and use the heat. Then the water can be pumped back down into the ground. It picks up more heat so the same water can be used again and again. This means it will never run out.

Keeping geothermal energy safe

In order to reach deep geothermal resources, rocks must be broken. Some people worry that this could cause destructive earthquakes. It does cause tiny earthquakes far underground. But they are rarely felt on the surface. Scientists can measure these tiny quakes. This helps them understand what's happening underground. International guidelines make sure the rocks aren't cracked too far. Special machines report any problems before the cracks get too large.

OTHER RENEWABLE ENERGY SOURCES

Geothermal power is not the only type of renewable energy. Other sources include solar and wind power. All of these energy sources are cleaner for the environment than fossil fuels. But geothermal is better in some ways. Solar and wind energy depend on sun and wind. Solar power stations can't make energy at night. Wind energy doesn't work well when the wind isn't blowing. Geothermal power plants can work all day and night. They can work every day, no matter the weather. They also take up less land than solar and wind power stations do.

One disadvantage is that geothermal energy won't work everywhere. It will take several forms of renewable energy to replace the power that fossil fuels make today. Solar power works best in sunny areas. Wind power needs strong, steady winds. Geothermal power needs hot water from underground. Hydropower works best where there is a large amount of flowing water.

Wind turbines tower over solar panels. Both generate renewable forms of energy, like geothermal power.

CHAPTER 4

WHO USES GEOTHERMAL POWER?

The Dieng Valley in Indonesia is the site of a geothermal power station.

As of January 2016, 24 countries were using geothermal power. Today, those with the highest number of geothermal plants include the United States, the Philippines, Indonesia and Mexico. Geothermal power is growing around the world. In 30 years, it could make up 10 to 20 per cent of the world's energy. So far, though, geothermal power has not been widely used. In 2015, it supplied less than 1 per cent of the world's energy.

Some western parts of the United States use geothermal energy. Earth's crust is thin or cracked in more places there. California produces the most geothermal energy. In other parts of the country, the crust is too thick to easily access geothermal energy. It would be difficult and expensive to reach deep geothermal resources. Because of that, less than 1 per cent of the United States' energy use comes from geothermal power. Even so, that's enough power for 3 million people.

FUNDING ALTERNATIVES

Most energy still comes from fossil fuels. You may wonder why, when renewable energy is better for the planet. Building new power stations costs a lot of money. It's easier and less expensive in the short term to keep using the old stations. But in the long term, it's a change that needs to happen for the good of all people and the planet.

Government support can help pay for new power stations. Many countries help fund both renewable energy and the fossil fuel industry. But fossil fuels get much more government money than renewable energy. Giving more money towards developing renewable resources would reduce pollution and help fight climate change.

Government support can help solve other challenges too. The conditions needed for a geothermal power station aren't common. Some areas are too cold or too dry. In other places the water can't move through the rock. Government funding could help companies design new systems. They might find ways to work around these challenges.

Building new power stations can cost billions of pounds. Government funding can help towards those costs.

CHAPTER 5

LOOKING TO THE FUTURE

In geothermal district heating, cool water is sent to great depths. There it heats up. The rising steam is converted to energy. These systems may become more common in the future.

1000 meter

What does the future hold for geothermal energy? New technology is being developed that could bring geothermal power to more areas. Some places have enough heat but not enough water. Or the water they have is trapped under solid rock. It's hard to drill down to that water. Enhanced geothermal systems could get to it. The systems shoot water into small cracks in the ground. This widens the cracks. Then water can move through the rock. As it rises, it gains heat from the warm rocks. The water becomes hot enough to make electricity.

RECYCLED WELLS

Old oil wells might be able to make new geothermal power. Thousands of oil wells are no longer used. They are deep enough to reach high temperatures underground. Scientists believe it's possible that water or steam pumped through these wells could be used to make power. This would be cheaper than drilling new wells.

Reusing old oil wells for geothermal power would be an environmentally friendly way to create new power.

OTHER OPTIONS

Some places may have water but not enough heat. Then, lower-temperature systems can work. These **binary** cycle systems use groundwater that is less than 205°C (400°F). This fluid heats a second (binary) fluid in a heat exchanger. The second fluid boils at a much lower temperature than water. When it boils, the steam turns the blades in the turbine. These systems are also good for the planet. They put nothing into the air except water. About half of all current geothermal power plants use this system. There may be more in the future.

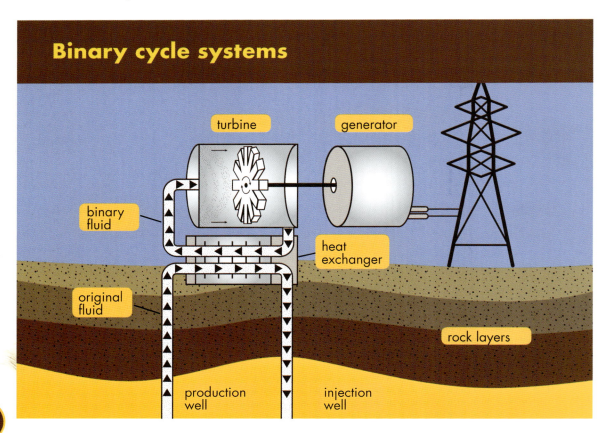

Binary cycle systems

turbine

generator

binary fluid

heat exchanger

original fluid

rock layers

production well

injection well

The future may also see more **cascading** geothermal projects. This process uses the same fluid several times. First, the fluid is used to make electricity. At this point the fluid is cooling but still warm. The system then provides heat and hot water. That can provide enough heat for certain uses. For example, the warm fluid could be used to keep greenhouses warm. It could also be pumped through pipes under pavements in cold countries to melt snow.

binary made up of two parts or units

cascade series of steps in a process where each step depends on the previous steps

Imperial Valley, California, USA, is the site of a binary geothermal power station.

GEOTHERMAL HEAT PUMP SYSTEMS

In some places, people can't reach hot underground water no matter what. Yet buildings can still use the earth's heat. Three metres (10 feet) below the ground, the soil stays about the same temperature all the time. Throughout the year, that temperature is 7°C (45°F) to 21°C (75°F). That's often warmer than the air temperature in winter. In the summer, the ground is cooler than the air temperature.

A geothermal heat pump system makes use of the temperature difference between the air and the ground. Pipes containing fluid are buried underground. The fluid becomes the same temperature as the ground around the pipes. A pump exchanges heat between the earth and a building. In the winter, it pulls heat from underground to heat a building. In the summer, the pump can move heat from the building back into the ground. Geothermal heat pumps cost a bit more to install than ordinary heating units. But they save 40 to 60 per cent on heating and cooling costs each year. They are also the best heating and cooling systems for the environment. They release fewer than half the amount of greenhouse gases than other systems.

A geothermal heat pump warms a shopping centre.

FACT

The geothermal energy industry is growing fast. In the United States, 60,000 new geothermal heat pumps are installed each year.

GEOTHERMAL AND YOU

Does working with geothermal energy sound interesting to you? You may want to study engineering. An **engineer** is someone who designs and builds machines. Geothermal power stations employ many engineers.

The geothermal industry also needs scientists. Geothermal resources are not always easy to find. Geologists are scientists who study the earth. They can help to work out what's happening underground. Chemists are scientists who can help find geothermal resources by studying the chemicals in well water.

What will the future bring? Geothermal energy could provide much more power to the world than it does now. Many countries could get all of their power from geothermal energy. But for that, we'll need better systems. That requires people with creativity who can solve problems.

People who work with geothermal power help to keep our world running. They do it in a way that is kind to our planet. Could you be one of those people?

....

engineer person who uses science and maths to plan, design or build

Chemists study water samples to look for chemicals that could mean there is geothermal activity in an area.

GLOSSARY

ancient from a long time ago

binary made up of two parts or units

cascade series of steps in a process where each step depends on the previous steps

climate change significant change in Earth's climate over a period of time

engineer person who uses science and maths to plan, design or build

generator machine used to convert mechanical energy into electricity

geothermal relating to the intense heat inside the earth

hydropower form of energy caused by flowing water

renewable power from sources that will not be used up, such as wind, water and sun

turbine machine with blades that can be turned by steam or water

FIND OUT MORE

BOOKS

Energy (Essential Physical Science), Louise and Richard Spilsbury (Raintree, 2014)

From Crude Oil to Fast Food Snacks: An energy journey through the world of heat (Energy Journeys), Ian Graham (Raintree, 2016)

How Renewable Energy Works (Eco Works), Geoff Barker (Franklin Watts, 2017)

WEBSITES

www.bbc.com/bitesize/articles/ztxwqty
Learn more about renewable and non-renewable energy.

www.dkfindout.com/uk/science/electricity/generating-electricity
Find out more about how electricity is generated and different sources of energy.

DISCUSSION QUESTIONS

1. Do you think geothermal power would work well where you live? Why or why not?

2. Many different fields of science are involved in the geothermal industry. Which is more interesting to you – engineering, chemistry or geology? Why?

3. Geothermal power does not work well everywhere. New technology could bring it to more areas. Should we support new geothermal technology? Or should time and money go to different forms of energy? Why?

INDEX